You can't Bullshit a Bull!

a Jesus Story

by

Larry A. Yff

Sometimes I start a book off with a round-a-bout apology. I let the Reader know that my view is all about God, Jesus and the Holy Spirit and that, so I don't lose anyone who doesn't believe in God or that Jesus is who He said He is, you, Reader, won't zone out early on and miss an important message.

This time is different. I'm going to be bold like I know how to do and that means yes, yes this book is about Jesus, I love Jesus and since He was as bold as a bull, I can now live my life as bold as a bull and you will not be able to bullshit me. The only question left to answer is: do I start with the bull or the bullshit?

Let's start with the bull since that's what the title of the book is based off of and then we'll get into the bullshit...

The bull is a powerful animal. Once it sees his target, there is no running away from it. I mean, you can run away from it, but you'd better run fast and not slow and you better be prepared to keep that pace for a long-ass time.

I saw that thing called the Bull Run over in Spain or Mexico or Guatemala one time. They release a bunch of bulls and they run down the street of a town chasing a bunch of idiots who actually want to get run over and trampled by the crowd of bulls! What in the fuck?

I guess it's an honor to have one of those monsters gut you with their horns. I don't see anything fun about a bull running me over and stomping my skull into the concrete, but, whatever…

I'm not sure if it's a myth or not, but apparently when a bull sees something red, he will move all kind of shit out the way to get to it. Once he gets to it, I don't know if his goal is to eat it, look at it or stomp on it. I don't even know if the bull knows what he wants to do with his red target.

I think that's where the saying, "like a bull in a China shop" comes from. Basically, what that saying means is if you let a bull run loose in a shop that sells a bunch of glasses and breakable shit, he will lose his mind. He will lose focus and tear up everything in there and the more noise and glass-breaking he hears, the more amped up he gets and the more he will continue to tear shit up.

I say Jesus has that bull mentality because His entire life's work was about the Kingdom of Heaven and He stayed locked on that target and didn't let anybody get in His way. The thing about Jesus was that His physical strength isn't what gave Him His bull mentality. It was the spiritual aspect of life, in particularly Heaven and God, that was His power source.

There was an incident where Jesus was like a bull in a China shop that was documented. He had gone to the local temple and there were people buying and selling animals, pottery and pussy. Jesus was pissed!

He was so mad, He took the time to grab some strands of rope, tie them together, make a whip and then started to whip all the vendors and kicking their tables over! He was *literally* whippin' they asses and telling them His Father's house was not a fuckin' swap meet or a place for temple prostitutes.

That's bold! That takes balls! That takes bull-balls! That was an intentional, planned act of violence. It wasn't like He came into the temple and started attacking the vendors...He plotted and was patient.

The Bible says, "...and He took some chords of rope and made a whip..." That's a significant point to talk about. That means He walked in and wasn't happy with what He saw, but He didn't lose His temper. He took the time to slow down, find some chords, sit there and tie them all together and *then,* started whippin' ass.

Even though this is the only recorded act of Him using physical strength, He knew it was spiritual strength that was His real source of power. He understood the immense power He had access to as a human by daily tapping into the same spiritual power source we now have access to. Everyday He took time to pray, chat and get instructions from God.

He was constantly being confronted by people accusing Him of being a liar or that He was allied with Satan somehow. He didn't care. He didn't care and He was willing to openly accept all challengers and matadors in any arena at any time.

All of His parables were about Heaven.   He constantly tried to teach us about the powers of Kingdom citizenship, how we can get it and what it looks like. By tapping into this power, He was able to cure any disease, raise people from the dead, tell powerful demons to bow down like they were toddlers, stand His ground in the face of any adversity and He was pretty much being an all-around bad-ass!

He was letting us know through His earthly example, that we could and we needed to be able to do everything He was doing. He instructed us to tap into this power through daily prayer like He did. The Lord's Prayer is a powerful, legal petition.

Have you ever really looked at it? Maybe you have, but I just want to break it down a little because this daily petition is the legal piece of the puzzle that will help you get access to the power Jesus was talking about. Here it is:

1. **Our Father:** Jesus is letting us know we need to view God as a father and not just any father. God is OUR father. We have power in numbers. He said, "...and wherever 2 or more of you are gathered and requesting something of me, you are guaranteed to get it." Jesus already identified God as His father and wanted us to view God in the same way.

2. **Who is in Heaven:** Jesus is letting us know even though God is omnipresent, or present everywhere, He is still a being. He is a being who is in a particular place. This is important in getting personal with God. Viewing God as

being some mysterious cloud who is everywhere can be tricky. I used to imagine Him as being some sort of unseen mist that covered the entire universe somehow and it was hard for me to get personal with a mist and call the mist "Father".

3. **Hallowed be thy name:** That's a fancy, churchy word that means respect. When you include this part of the prayer, you are acknowledging that not only is the being God respected, but even His name is respected. I used to say "goddammit" when I would get extra mad. I am extremely careful about letting that word slip out of my mouth now. When I do, I instantly catch myself, apologize for disrespecting God and sinning, ask that my sin be legally taken off the books based on Jesus legally conquering sin...and then I sit back and shut the fuck up so I don't get in any more trouble with God.

4. **Thy Kingdom come and thy will be done on Earth as it is in Heaven:** We are asking for 2 powerful things here. The

1st is that we are asking God to establish Heaven on Earth.
The 2nd thing is that we are acknowledging how God works
because God legally gave control of the world systems and
the Earth to humans. Since we're in control, He can't just
legally come in on His own and correct stuff. He is legally
bound to wait until He is asked by humans to intervene in
human affairs. The 3rd thing is we are putting ourselves in
positions of powers. Whoever is petitioning God to come
is in essence asking God to work through him or her to
establish Heaven on Earth. That person is positioning him
or her self to have the creator of the universe personally
bless him/her with earthly and Heavenly resources to
establish the Kingdom of Heaven on Earth! If God puts it
on you to fix corruption in politics...He will give you all the
resources you need to have the financial resources to oust
lobbyist from tampering with our political systems! If God
puts it on you to correct the education system...He will

give you all the resources you need to buy and maintain new schools!

5. **Give us this day our daily bread:** We are not only asking God to position us as influencers on Earth, we are also asking and acknowledging Him as being our daily source. When I pray this part, I add," ...whatever daily bread may be whether it's gas for the car, food in the fridge, Planet Fitness membership to keep my body healthy..."

6. **And forgive us our trespasses:** Jesus hadn't yet legally paid the human-blood wage for sin, so for me, I take the liberty to not ask that God forgives our sins, I say, "...and thank you for legally forgiving our sins with your Jesus plan..." It is a personal acknowledgement on my part that what Jesus did was part of a God-backed plan and I'm also acknowledging the legal aspect of what Jesus did. This forgiveness still requires action on my part: I have to acknowledge what I did was a sin to God and then acknowledge it was Jesus who paid the price for sin and

then I can ask for my sin to be taken off the record books

legally.

7. **Lead us not into temptation and deliver us from evil and the evil one.** Once again, I took the liberty to thank God for His "Jesus" plan that delivered us from evil. Remember, Jesus hadn't yet done that when He was telling people how they should pray and what they should ask for. I also include, "...do not lead us into temptation because we can get there all by ourselves without any help..."

And that's pretty much what we need to do everyday to keep tapped into our power source. This daily action has helped me overcome addictions, delivered me from feeling hopeless and like I was just some piece-of-shit drug addict and opened me up to be positioned as one of Heaven's influencers on Earth.

Starting my day off like this reminds me, before I even start worrying or plotting and planning what the fuck I wanna do for the day, that 1) I'm not here to follow my own agenda and 2)

I'm legally bound out of respect to follow God's agenda and when

I do that, I can relax.

I can relax because Jesus told us to have the confidence to

live one day at a time. That's powerful! To be able to enjoy each

day and not worry or give a fuck about what happened yesterday

or what might happen today means you are confident! You are a

fucking bull!

Hey, Reader. Can you honestly say you walk around with

your chest out or your head held high knowing everything is

gonna be all good? I'm not talking about walking around saying,

"I know God has my back. I'm not even going to worry about it. I

just have to give it all to Him even though it's hard."

What I'm talking about is you walking around saying,

"What am I supposed to be worried about?" when you ain't got

no job, don't know where your next dollar is coming from and people are talking shit about you. I'm talking about keeping this mentality when you may not even know what God's plans are for you and you don't know what to plan because you don't know what you're supposed to be doing in this particular season.

I said that to get a little personal with you, reader. My wife and I have walked a faith walk for the past couple years. We haven't worked 9-5 jobs because we feel like God is allowing us time to bond as a husband and wife, work on other close relationships and work on the books and other plans He gave us to do.

While we're in this process, I'm walking around with my head high and people are getting mad at me. How can you walk around so confident when you aren't working? How can you take care of your family without working? Why don't you have any plans? What are you gonna do? Why are you having another baby when you're broke?

We can be as confident as bulls because what you see isn't always what you got or are gonna get. There's a spiritual side of life that few people take time to pay attention to. God has allowed us this opportunity during this time and like I shared with you earlier, "...when you are focused 1st and foremost on establishing Heaven on Earth and have asked God to help you fulfill this task, you are listening to His guiding voice and you are relying on Him for you daily needs...", you don't have to make plans. You don't have to worry...so we don't make plans and we don't worry.

The daily Lord's Prayer means I don't have to worry about money or food. I asked God to provide me with whatever could be classified as "daily bread" for that day. If I need money, then HE HAS TO PROVIDE IT FOR ME ON THAT DAY!!! Yes, He literally has to provide whatever I need for that day and if I don't get it, then my black-ass didn't need it that day!

I forgot something. There is one, little catch: you have to

be working on establishing Heaven on Earth. When you prayed

the daily prayer, you were asking God to help you establish

Heaven on Earth…NOT to make sure your company makes money

and you ain't using the profits towards establishing Heaven! You

can't get mad when your bank account isn't growing when you're

not tithing the full 10% and you're trying to get money to take

care of you, your needs, your family, your kids and your house.

Big difference, there.

Here's some good news for you. If you are focusing on

"seeking 1st the Kingdom of God", then as you go about your daily

business, everything you, your family, your kids and your house

need will all be taken care of. It's guaranteed to be taken care of

because God will do whatever it takes to make sure you're not

chasing the American Dream or any other get-rich-quick scams.

He has to make sure He keeps His word just like we have

to keep our word. Keeping His word means since we're asking

Him to take of our daily needs like Jesus told us to ask…He's legally bound to do that.

That's good news on a personal level. You are needed by God to be an influencer and that looks different for everybody. One person may need to influence the children at a daycare, while another may need to be an influence at home and another could be needed to be an influencer at a fast-food restaurant with the other food staff.

How about some good news for the entrepreneurs out there? If you have a company and you're pumping resources into establishing Heaven on Earth and using the resources He's providing you with in that manner, you won't run out of shit!

Since you're letting the world know you are a company that is operating under God's law, will and influence, it is in God's best interest to make sure it's the most valuable, profitable company the world has ever seen! His reputation is on the line, so put Him to the test!

How's that for a power move! You can operate a multi-billion-dollar company if that's in your plans to take over an earthly industry and put it under Heaven's rule.

If you believe God put some major plans for Heaven in your life and you don't have a college degree…it doesn't matter!

If you believe God put some major plans for Heaven in your life and you don't have a job or money in the bank…it doesn't matter!

If you believe God put some major plans for Heaven in your life and you have felonies…it doesn't matter!

If you believe God put some major plans for Heaven in your life and you just got a divorce and are trying to make life work for you and your kids by yourself…it doesn't matter!

Don't shit matter as it relates to needing resources if you're operating with a daily mindset of establishing Heaven on Earth. You now have the capacity to be bold as a bull!

I'm talking about this because I like to "write the vision down and make it plain" like we are instructed to do by one of the authors in the Bible. With that being said, God has put it on my heart to do certain things and I had to write them down. Here are a couple of them:

- Write books that give God glory and have the ability to reach audience around the world and share what He has done in my life AND how it can work for them.

- Take over entire cities and have them turned around to look and operate like Heaven's influence is there and guess what? I believe it will happen even though I don't have enough money right now to go to rent a bird-house!

- Take over the entire public school system and get God's name back in it and guess what? I believe it will happen even though I don't have enough money right now to buy

a piece of paper or a pencil!

I could go on and on with the plans He gave me, but I

won't. The point is, I live every day like I'm a fuckin' bull! I'm

chasing after the plans God has for me like I'm the bull chasing the

stupid-asses intentionally running down the street in front of me

wearing bright, red t-shirts during Bull Week in Spain!

I'm living every day like I got the financial resources right

now to purchase and takeover all the shit God wants me to

takeover and manage for Him!

I'm living every day like I'm ready to bum-rush anybody in

my way today and I'm able to do that because I understand true

power! Having the backing of the Creator of the universe, the

King of Kings on Earth and the Holy Spirit...any territory I'm

coming for will not be able to resist my takeover!

Alright, we gotta change subjects or I'll get completely off track and you don't need me to do that, so, let's get back to talking about bulls…

There is something else I want to share with you, Reader, because a lot of Christians have a misconception about Jesus, even lifetime members Christians and I wanna clear some shit up.

The word on the street is Jesus is the Holy, meek and mild Lamb. He is the gentle Shepherd. He is lowly and humble at times and all of that is true but don't get it twisted! Don't make any mistakes about it: God is a God of war and so is His Son and so should we!

Jesus said, "I didn't come here for peace! I came with the sword! I'm here to legally reclaim the world systems for humanity! Whoever is with me is with me and will be rewarded in this life and the next. Whoever is against me is against me and will be punished in this life and the next. I don't care if siding with me means you wind up going against your mother, father,

brother, sister, child, husband or wife! You better do what you

gotta do if you wanna roll with me!"

Raging Bull or Mild Lamb? You decide...

I am a lion lover and it pains me to watch them face-off

with bulls in the wild. It pains me because lions will back down.

Not some of the time...all of the time. Even when they have

strength in numbers, they know when you put the power, brute

strength and mentality of a bull together it could easily spell death

for the lion or lions.

It's funny because some big, powerful male lions, for

instance, may separate a water buffalo from the herd and even

bring it down. The bulls in the herd don't care. They will still

come back to their fallen comrade and chase the lions away and

they can do this all day long.

No matter how many big male lions are on kill, they

scatter like cockroaches. They know how irritated the powerful

bulls can get so they all play a game where the bulls rush forward

and the they retreat. Then they growl and rush forward and the

bull's retreat. In the end, the lions get their meat, the bulls leave

their dead friend with the lions and everybody goes on about the

business of eating or being eaten.

That's bulls in the wild. Remember we talked about

domestic bulls? I want to touch on that one more time before we

get into the bullshit aspect of this book...

Have you ever watched a bull fight with a matador? I have

and it's amazing how aggressive the bull is. He's aggressive as

fuck even though there's a 99% chance he will eventually lose.

I think the percentage is super high, maybe not 99%, but

it's high enough to know that any bull in his right mind should try a different strategy or maybe just sit there and let the matador

just kill him already without all the extra running around.

Once a bull enters the arena, all he sees is the matador

and a red flag and that's all he wants to fuck up: the matador and

the red flag. Nothing else matters. The bull can miss the red flag

a thousand times as the matador spins it away from him and

sticking him with a sharp knife and the bull doesn't give a shit.

He will continue to chase the matador and the flag over

and over until the bull gets tired and the matador kills it or the

bull manages to kill the matador.

I'm talking about a bull instead of some other cattle-

examples like a lamb, because Jesus had more of a bull mentality,

but He had it with an advantage: He knew the outcome! He knew

He was in a life and death type of battle, but He also knew 1) the

"matador" didn't stand a chance of winning and 2) He, Jesus, was the one in control of the contest from the beginning because of

His relationship with God.

Every chance Jesus got to heal someone…He healed them.

Every chance Jesus got to kick a demon's ass…He kicked it.

Every chance Jesus got to let the religious leaders of the

day know they were full of shit and that He knew they were full of

shit…He told them.

Jesus is that bull in the arena and the arena is the world's

systems and the matador is Satan, well, kind of. I'm trying to

paint a picture for you, but it's not exactly like the bull in the

arena for Jesus.

1st off, the matador's job is to eventually kill the bull. He

teases the bull for hours until it gets tired and then it kills it. I

know I said Satan is like the matador, but He directly tested Jesus

one time and that was in the wilderness while Jesus was fasting

for 40 days.

Satan didn't tease or tempt Jesus for too long. On one occasion he tried to tempt Jesus 3 times when Jesus was at His weakest. They were in the wilderness somewhere when this happened and Jesus was on the 40th day of His 40-day fast.

Even in that weakened state of being, Jesus told Satan to get the fuck on and get the fuck out of his face. Satan left immediately. Even though Satan isn't directly taunting Jesus to His face like a matador, he is running around behind the scenes doing whatever it takes to get people to not pay attention to Jesus.

He's playing this deadly game every day, but unlike the bull-matador example, Satan knows his time is limited and that he has already lost and that he will lose every time. As the bull, Jesus knows His power. He knows His power and wanted us to power-up and get on His level.

Jesus knew all of this and passed this mentality on to anyone who believes in Him and His life and what He represents. Once I understood His bull mentality...there was no way you could bullshit me and try and make me think He isn't who He is or that He didn't do what historically accurate documents and eyewitness accounts from our present time and ancient times tell us He did.

Jesus knew it would be hard for anybody to understand who He was. How do you explain Heaven? How do you explain being the Son of God? How do you explain coming from Heaven to Earth? How do you explain being old enough to have witnessed Satan get kicked out of Heaven?

He knew it was a difficult task and told His 12 closest companions about this dilemma. They walked with Him on a daily basis for years, witnessed His miracles and were able to learn stuff directly from His mouth and they still didn't completely understand Him.

There was no mix-up in the messages they got…they still didn't get it all the time.

There was no NIV, KJV or ESV that gave the disciples His message with different wording…they still didn't get it all the time.

There were no translation issues from His language to theirs because they all spoke the same language. He didn't have to say it in Hebrew, get a translator to translate it to them in Greek and then have a Greek translator translate it back to Hebrew for Him to see if they understood what He was saying…and they still didn't get it all the time.

He talked to them as directly as possible, but He chose to talk in parables to everyone else. These parables let all of us in on the secrets to His power as well as how we can tap into this power for ourselves!

I'm sure you may have heard about His parables if you read the Bible, but if you have, I want you to still pay attention because I might present it to with an angle you aren't aware of or have ever seen. If you don't know about His parables, pay attention and learn some power stuff that Bible believers already have access to and now you will too!

99% of His messages were about the Kingdom of Heaven. Since Heaven is a spiritual place, He knew it would be hard to grasp so He put them in parables, which are kind of like a cross between a true story and a riddle with a storyline they could relate to.

All of His parables were power-based and in this form, because it made it easier for the masses to access the power. The simpler He could break His message of the Kingdom down, the more people would be able to have a better chance to comprehend it and put it into action. Here's a couple of examples for you:

In the parable of the rich man, Jesus started off like He always did and said, "The Kingdom of Heaven is like this…" and "The Kingdom of Heaven is like that…" In this example, He started off with, "The Kingdom of Heaven is like a rich man who had to leave where he was at and go to another country where he would be crowned King and then come back.

While he was gone, he gave a couple of his trusted servants some money to manage. When he returned, 2 of the servants double the money and were told their reward would be they would be in charge of many cities; while the 3rd servant played it safe and didn't do shit with the money. He didn't want to take the gamble and invest in the stock market and assumed the rich man would be happy that at least he didn't lose the money he was in charge of.

The 3rd servant was wrong. The rich man kicked that servant off the property and told him he wasn't worth shit and that's the end of the parable."

Ready for the power part? Ready for the bull mentality?

Jesus is telling people who believe in Him:

1. He is here on Earth, but He has to leave Earth, just like the

    rich man had to leave, and become King. Jesus knew He

    was destined to be King, so He wasn't worried about any

    obstacles and haters in His way. He knew He had to leave

    and that He would be King and that there was nothing or

    no one who could stop Him. **Power Principle: if nobody**

    can stop Jesus from completing His mission of controlling

    all the kingdoms and countries of the Earth and make

    them all function like Heaven functions, then nobody can

    stop any of us as we follow His laws while we're doing

    our part to establish Heaven on Earth. The key is that

    we have to be doing Kingdom business. We do that,

    whatever we get into will be a success!

2. When He is crowned the King, He is going to reward

    everybody who believed in Him and followed His laws. In

the parable, the rich man put them in charge of a lot of

cities based on the way each of them handled His money.

Jesus wasn't talking about money though. The currency

He was talking about wasn't money. It never is in His

parables. He knew we understand principles of money, so

He was applying it to His Kingdom message. He was

saying that He was entrusting people who believe in Him

with the knowledge of Heaven so they can operate on

Earth as effectively and productively as possible. You may

not necessarily be put in charge of many cities, but you

will be put in the position where you have control and

influence over some major areas on Earth that need

Kingdom guidance. One of the keys to this success is

understanding what Heaven is like. Remember, He was

always saying, "...the Kingdom of Heaven..." is like this or

that. So, in the case of this parable, He was telling the

masses if you believe in Him, He will give you all this

spiritual information about being a citizen of Heaven so

that you are able to enjoy this life by living out your God-given purpose. **Power Principle: You have to be close enough to Him so that He can present this spiritual information to you, 1ˢᵗ off. If you want access to the spiritual power He had, you need to get personal with Him. Once you are personal with Him, THAT is the key that gives you access to the power He had on Earth. Now, once you are close to Him and He trusts with you with the knowledge of this kind of power, you aren't off the hook. Remember the servant who didn't do shit with the money he was entrusted with? Well, if Jesus entrusts you with this Kingdom information and you don't do shit with it, He will consider you to be, in His words, "lazy and evil". You will also lose any position you thought you had in the Kingdom and in God's plans for establishing Heaven on Earth. The good news is all you have to do is apply the wisdom and information He breaks down and trusts you with from your devotionals**

and Bible studies towards establishing Heaven on Earth and you are golden! You are set! You are in good shape because now you can become a bull! You become aggressive in establishing Heaven because you understand who the King is and you understand the King is your brother and you understand that anything you get into is backed up based on the power and authority of your brother King...so can't shit stop you, Reader! You are royalty! I guess you could even say you would officially be a royal bull.

What I just showed you is a ton of power and confidence you can have, as someone who loves Jesus and shows it by applying His teachings in your life towards establishing Heaven. It is a type of legal power the world can't stop and it's backed by other-worldly powers. You can't lose, Reader!

Do you know what suicide is? Suicide is when a person gives up. He or she feels like he or she has no control or power over his or her life. It is also the result of feeling like you have no purpose. The roots of these can show appear as though it's from loss of a job, a divorce or a heartbreak situation.

That's actually superficial or surface shit. The real shit. The undercurrent is a separation between our physical and spiritual being. I think it's common for any of us to get frustrated when we aren't doing what we feel like we are capable of.

For me, even when I was making some good money doing different jobs or hustles and on the outside it may have looked like I had my shit together, I was still depressed. I was depressed because even though what I was doing was bringing in money, it wasn't me. It didn't complete me.

I took the escape route of drug addiction and that led to porn addiction. I didn't want to deal with reality and the fantasy world of drugs and pornos was an arena where I felt the most at home. I was comfy there and the physical and mental costs became irrelevant: I just wanted to forget reality for a couple of minutes or hours or day.

When I would get high and escape, I wanted it to last as long as possible no matter what the costs.

If I had a weekend trip planned…I didn't give a fuck. I wanted to escape reality and the trip could wait.

My wife needed the van to take the kids to school…I didn't give a fuck. I wanted to escape reality and her, the van, kids and the school could all wait.

The money I was using to get high was supposed to be towards the rent…I didn't give a fuck. I wanted to escape reality so the rent could wait.

As I began to get closer to God, I was able to take-in the plans He had for me. I was able to feel like I was worth something if the creator of the universe wanted to use me! I didn't want to get high anymore and block my messages from Him or fuck up my relationship with Him. Prior to that awareness though, I was dead.

What I want you to see is that even though I obviously didn't commit suicide, I was killing myself. I was killing myself because I was a dead man walking. What I knew I was built for and what I was doing wasn't adding up and that is death.

There are some scriptures and manuscripts that talk about how separation from God is like death. I didn't understand it until I experienced it for myself and I think many people don't and don't get the chance to search for life and they would rather end it. They would rather end it or do like I did and lose my shit to addictions.

I'm saying a lot of mental health issues are the direct result of a separation of spirit and body due to the separation of following God's laws versus our own, human laws and preferences. We see evidence of this in the news.

I've heard of many stories where an extremely wealthy person, who has all the health, sex, houses, boats and cars money could buy, still commit suicide or they weren't happy. Why not?

Why aren't you happy when you have the financial means to buy a small country, hire all its inhabitants, have sex with any of them you want and have the biggest yacht, the most expensive airplane and a French poodle named Regan dressed in Prada?

A lot of them, even with all the wealth feel a certain kind of emptiness or deadness in side. Look at Bill Gates. He is consistently one of the wealthiest people on the planet and has amassed billions of dollars and now, towards the end of his life in an attempt to be at peace and find purpose in life, has decided to give away all of his wealth.

He worked long hours for his entire life to get all this wealth and he just wants to give it all away as a show of purpose? He even got his good friend Warren Buffett, another one who stays in the top 10 wealthiest people on the planet, to do the same.

It's like they became blood brothers and now that they're both about to be 90, they've decided the key to finding purpose in life is to give away all your wealth so humanity. Bullshit! I call bullshit! We're not even into the part of bullshit yet, but I call bullshit!

You want to wait until your ass is too old to enjoy the money doing fun shit and then tell everyone having money isn't a good thing, huh?

You want to wait until you've had fun with your billions, taken care of your family with billions, bought anything you've ever wanted with your billions, purchased millions of acres of farmland and then, then you want to tell people money isn't everything, right?

You want to wait until you're too old to enjoy travelling and having sex to say, "You know what? The key to life is to give away all your money. I've realized this and I want to share my wealth and this knowledge to the whole world and make it a better place."

You're both full of shit! In reality, these 2 didn't really *give away all their wealth.* If you'll notice they were only talking about the paper money. The money on the books. Bill ain't talking about giving up the millions of acres of farmland he's been secretly buying through fake corporations and Warren ain't talking about giving up any of his physical assets like his insurance companies and real estate holdings...

What Bill Gates did was take all his wealth from his personal pockets and transferred it all to his personal, charitable organization that he still basically controls. What about his buddy Warren? Well, Warren is giving all of his money "away" too. He's promised to give it all to Bill's private organization as well!

In attempts to try and make sense out of life and give back to the world and make humanity a better place, these two have chosen to take billions of their personal wealth and put it in an account they both control; meanwhile, they're fully aware of the tax benefits of "donating" billions of dollars and the control they will still have over that money.

Why am I going on and on about 2 old rich guys? It's because they both don't believe in God and their attempts to "get right" are based on all physical, money-based solutions. The world is watching and believes that's the best way to do it and are being misled by these 2 influencers in society.

So, if having billions of dollars doesn't give you life and purpose and giving away billions of dollars doesn't give your life meaning and purpose, there has to be something else to get you to that goal and it's something money can't buy, right?

That's where we circle back to Jesus and the bull

mentality. Jesus understands the principles of money and wealth

and used them as examples in His parables to get us to

understand that it's not about the money. It never is.

The principal Jesus is sharing with us is the keys to life and

power have nothing to do with money and everything to do with

Heaven. Our purpose is not to get as much money, cars and

planes as we possibly can. Look at the example I just showed you

about Bill and Warren.

The key to having control and power over your life comes

when you take your eyes off of your personal gains and use

everything at your disposal towards establishing Heaven on Earth.

That's it and that's all. That is our purpose and that's what we

were designed for according to Jesus and the overwhelming

amount of evidence supports this.

Jesus was bold and aggressive in the face of Pontius Pilate, the governor who was supposed to have Him killed, because Jesus wasn't worried about his power. Jesus knew He had the spiritual power and backing of the creator of the universe, so He was able to talk to Pontius like He talked to anyone else.

Jesus was bold and aggressive in the face of the top religious leaders of the day because He knew the power He had behind Him was higher than the earthly power they were busy chasing.

Jesus was bold and aggressive in the face of death and every situation and He wants us to be the same. He said He wanted to build His church on power: the power of His name and authority.

He said He was going to make His church body so powerful that death, demons and any other enemy of His won't stand a chance. With that being said, I'm wondering what He's thinking

about the condition of our version of what a church is.

I personally think He would be disgusted, but I'm not

gonna go there right now either. "Please Poke the Bear! – a

Church Story" is a book that goes into a lot more detail about my

views on all things churchy…

Now for some talk about the bullshit…

I watch documentaries, but I'm careful to not watch

certain ones. My favorite ones are about lions or business

tycoons, but I'm also open to religious ones. I'm always curious to

see what the opposition has to say about Jesus, who their

supposed experts are and what their supposed proof is.

The 1st thing I noticed was the content. I, like many

people, have been led to believe Islam and Muslims are terrorists

and don't give a fuck about life. Not their life. Not their victim's

lives. Not anybody's life. They're selfish.

I've been taught to think they are the enemy because they don't believe in God the way I, as a Christian do, and that's not fair. It's not fair, it's most likely completely false, it breeds hatred and gives anything spiritual a bad reputation.

If I was interested in Islam, after watching documentaries, I would say "fuck them". I don't care if, since I'm black and I'm supposed to support "black religion", it was the Nation of Islam: I'm not fucking with Muslims. I don't want to know them, eat with them, be friends with them or live near them. That would be my mentality.

Let mainstream media have their way, they would continue to show as much violence and ignorant aspects of religions and spiritual walks as possible. Why? Why and who is behind it and what would be gained?

Let's start with the "why"...

Large media companies make billions of dollars in advertising if they can get billions of people to watch their networks. People have been programmed to expect blood, guts, murder and controversy from the news sections of these companies.

I don't watch the news anymore. I know how it's gonna start and finish before I tune in to it and I'm not falling for the bullshit. What's gonna happen is they are going to say, "And in the news, a man was murdered in Philly, a child was raped in Utah, a dead body was found in the Detroit River and a child-sex-trafficking ring was discovered with high-ranking members of Congress caught in the sting...all this and more, coming up after these commercials..."

We are groomed to expect this kind of news. We are groomed to think the world is going to end. We are groomed to think humanity is evil and there is no good in the world. We are being groomed by Satan and anyone working with him to think religion and spirituality is a thing to be avoided.

I was raised in a predominantly white church in Grand Rapids Michigan. God, Jesus, angels and all the prophets had long, wavy blonde hair and blue eyes. All the pastors were white men. All the songs were written by white people and were melancholy, boring and very slow.

As I got older, I began to check out black churches. The pastors all shouted and talked like they were clearing their throats, the choir shouted when they sang and God, Jesus, the angels and all the prophets were depicted as being black or at least brown-skinned.

Either way, I fell for the bullshit. I was sick of God, religion and everything that had a hint of spirituality. Why? What was it? I wish I could blame it on the media, but I can't.

I mean, I can blame them for showing us all the religious bullshit, but it's not their fault. It's not their fault because they are simply giving the people what they want. We want excitement. We want to know about murders, house-burnings, rapes, violence and genocide. It acts as a sort of twisted affirmation that "our community isn't as bad as that community!"

Let's get away from murders and bloodshed and stay focused on the bullshit we're being told about religion and spirituality…

I am technically a Christian and I love God, Jesus and the Holy Spirit. From what I know, Muslims love their god and their prophets. Why should I hate them? Why shouldn't I be able to be cool with my fellow humans? Why am I being taught to hate anyone who doesn't follow my spiritual path?

I'm asking a lot of questions and not providing you with a lot of answers and there's a reason for that: I don't have all the answers. Religion has become a cluster-fuck of power-grabs.

You have the Catholic church with their Pope and the Virgin Mary. I personally think that's bullshit. I don't think the Pope should be viewed as having healing powers and shouldn't be worshipped like he is.

That old, mutha fucka has bull-time body guards and a $20-billion-dollar budget! What the fuck is really going on in the Catholic church! They are the largest and most valuable land-owners on the planet!

I like it, but I don't like it. I like the fact that a religious organization is setting itself up to be self-sufficient, but I'm not sure about the need for a lot of the other business dealings they are in and since I don't really have access to all that info...I'm not gonna speak on it.

Maybe I'm a little jealous?

Maybe I'm wishing the Christian church would start focusing more on being self-sustainable and less on getting people all excited and hyped up and in a giving mood once a week.

Maybe I'm wishing the pastor focused more on helping his flock become investors and less on them being tithers?

Maybe I just need to shut up if I'm not doing anything to help churches get to that financial position?

I came across a pastor who was proud of the fact that his church had a good enough credit score to get a loan to make some major repairs. What the fuck? Why hasn't the church positioned itself so it can bring in monthly revenue?

Then there's the Virgin Mary. I respect her. I respect the way she accepted her calling from an early age and interacted with angels without fear as a young girl. I love how she accepted her role and did the difficult task of handling a virgin birth quite well, BUT I don't like how she is worshipped and prayed to.

She is the mother, but Jesus is still the focus. I did some research on Mary and wondered why people worshipped her. I found out that she used to "sell" the bathwater of Jesus or His wash clothes when He was a baby to people who wanted His healing power.

They obviously couldn't ask Jesus, so they went to His mother. Mary was known for obliging them and in return, her and Joseph were praised, given monetary gifts and that led to her being worshipped to day still. Once again, I'm cool with acknowledging Mary, but I think it's bullshit to pray to her and have "Hail Mary" prayers and beads.

Let's pause really quickly because I want to make sure you understand what I'm saying. What I'm saying is I think human behavior surrounding religion and spirituality has become a bunch of bullshit and I'm not limiting it to Islam or the Catholic church.

I'm in the Christian religion and the bullshit I see that I hate is racial. I see white churches who swear up and down they love God and they love everyone...but they remain run by white people and are "white-themed" from the pastor to the extra-curricular activities such as retreats.

The black churches swear up and down they love God and they love everyone the way God told them to...but they remain run by white people and are "black-themed" from the pastor to the extra-curricular activities such as retreats.

It's all bullshit! Religion and spirituality are human things. Since we are all humans, why are we doing this thing based on skin color? There is already division based on spiritual path, so I see no need to add another, major element of division.

On one hand, I'm saying it's okay to be cool with people from other spiritual beliefs, but on the other hand, God was very clear and quick to tell the Israelites to not fuck with other religions. He said don't marry anyone with other religious beliefs and if you live in an area where "they" live, don't mix with them.

Even when it came to business transactions. God said the Israelites weren't supposed to charge each other interest, but they were supposed to charge foreigner's interest. So what is it?

Are we supposed to do our spiritual services apart and then come together somehow and build schools together or are we supposed to stay focused on our religious paths and only deal with other people who have the same spiritual beliefs?

Once again, I'm not a Bible scholar and I don't have multiple degrees in Bible stuff...I just have my own spiritual walk with my own results and I like to share them with whoever wants to listen or read about 'em. I want to share them because my views have made my life better and if somebody wants to give it a try, I welcome it.

In the beginning of this section, I talked about documentaries and then I switched and started talking about the media, then the news and then some other shit that had nothing to do with documentaries and that wasn't my intention. I wanted to talk some more about documentaries about the Bible because they are full of shit!

The host is full of shit!

The experts they call on are full of shit!

Their reasoning is full of shit!

Their evidence is full of shit!

Everything about every documentary or show I have seen on Christianity is full of shit and I don't want you to watch 'em. I would rather you just take my word for it and pay attention to the way they try and tear Christianity down.

Some of the stuff makes sense if you're not grounded in God and could maybe make you doubt a couple of things in the Bible and that can be a dangerous thing. All Satan needs is for you to doubt a little and he can get a foothold and fuck up the rest of your life and the life of your kids…if you're not careful.

One of the things that makes these documentaries tricky is the hosts and the sources. The hosts and the sources don't believe in God, yet they have degrees in Bible-stuff?!? They have gotten these degrees, I guess, just to spend their life disproving it all and making it sound official.

Regarding their sources, they don't believe in God either. I guess since they have multiple degrees in history, and usually history in areas where a lot of the Bible stories played themselves out, they feel like they are qualified to disprove the Bible as well.

Then you have people like Bill Maher. He is a comedian.

This mutha fucka tells jokes for a living, but he went on a

"Christian tour" so he could make fun of and disprove Christianity.

Who the fuck is he? Does he have a theology degree or

something?

He doesn't have any of that shit. He tells jokes. He tells

jokes, but people who make money appear to be successful and

that breeds pride and influence. It breeds pride because they put

themselves in the position to tell everybody they made it on their

own with no mention of God and influence because the world

sees riches and wealth as a sign of influence and tend to believe

anything anybody with money says and that can be very

dangerous.

Alright, enough introduction to the documentaries, let me

show you what I've seen and let you know why I call bullshit:

1. **Feeding manna to the Israelites in the wilderness during the 40 years:** I believe the story where the credible author of that book in the Bible tells us the Israelites were fed daily by God. They were fed manna and something else, maybe Quail meat. The manna came down from the sky and covered the entire ground of the large camp where they stayed and they could only pick up enough for that day. Even if they tried to be sneaky and stash some for the next day, it wouldn't matter because it would automatically become moldy and un-edible after midnight. The host, who had accreditations in Bible history, said it wasn't God who provided the manna. His version is that the Ark of the Covenant was really some kind of cooking machine that spewed manna into the air. The Ark was basically a box. Maybe the size of a small coffin. It was a sacred box the Israelites had to always carry with them because God made His dwelling in it and there were some valuable, holy items inside it as well.

Only the High Priest could touch it. I can only liken it to

being like a snow machine that takes water, freezes it,

turns it to snow and then blows snow all over the place.

Can you believe that bullshit? It may be hard to believe

God somehow did it, but to say the Ark was some type of

dual-purpose oven that was capable of somehow baking

manna and then somehow blowing it into the sky,

covering the entire camp to allow 750,000 people to have

access to it! Bullshit! What I always noticed was that they

weren't so much denying the event happened; instead

they focused on disproving it. They risk credibility if they

say 1) the Bible story about the Israelites being in the

wilderness for 40 years was false and 2) there was no Ark

where God lived and 3) they weren't provided manna

every day. By not disproving those 3 points, they in fact

prove the events are historically accurate, they in fact

happened, God was with the Israelites and the Bible is

historically accurate.

2. **The walls of Jericho falling down.** The Israelites had to

attack a city called Jericho. Jericho is a real place and the

Israelites are real people and the battle really happened.

The host of the show even said he couldn't disprove the

event took place, but he was still out to prove it didn't

happen the way the Bible said it did. In this recorded

event, the Israelites had to attack this city, but God told

them to not use military force. He told the army leader to

instruct the soldiers to march around the city 7 times a

day for 3 days blowing trumpets and on the 3rd day the

walls would collapse and then they could run in there and

kill everybody and take all their valuable shit. This was

more of a faith mission than a military one. They followed

their leader, marched around the city and just like God

said, the walls fell down on the 3rd day and the Israelite

army had a victory. Now, the host knows about the

event, but he said the event couldn't have taken place like

that and he had proof. He said around the time of the

attack, there was also a massive earthquake in that region and it was a coincidence that on Day Three, the earthquake just so happened to hit and knock the walls of Jericho down. Bullshit! It's bullshit and here's why: 1st off, he is acknowledging another historically accurate event that is described in the Bible as being true, but he's just changing the storyline. He's trying to say a natural earthquake happened on Day Three and you know what? I can accept that. I can accept that because maybe God did use a massive earthquake to shake the walls down. The bottom line is they trusted God enough to march around the walls and not use their own military strength and believed on the 3rd days the walls would crumble somehow or other. So, once again, in trying to disprove something, he's actually supporting the Bible! There were recorded events where God spoke through a cloud and it had the same effect as an earthquake. Apparently, the power in His voice shook the ground that much.

3. **Noah's Ark and the flood.** There was a massive flood sent

by God during history to flood the whole Earth.

Apparently, the entire 1st round of humanity was fucking

up pretty badly and there were also huge, man-eating

giants on the Earth called Nephilim. God contacted a man

named Noah, told him to build an ark and then, once a

male and female of every animal entered the ark, God

was gonna close the door and flood everything. Only

Noah, his family and the animals on board would survive

to repopulate the Earth in Round Two. This host said

there was no way the Earth could have completely

flooded, but if you look at the Grand Canyon in the United

States and mountain ranges all around the world, there is

proof of a massive flood. There have been flood-lines

found on very high mountain tops. Flood-lines are

basically water lines. They are what remains after water

has gone down. I worked on Hurricane Katrina clean-up

and saw these lines on the insides and outsides of houses

and buildings. You can see how high the water was and you can see the different lines below those showing the different times the water went down and stayed at that level. I don't remember his proof, but I do remember him saying it was impossible to flood the whole Earth.

4. **Jonah and the whale.** There was a man named Jonah who lived thousands of years ago. He was supposed to go to a city called Nineveh and give them a message from God. For whatever reason, he didn't want to go. In fact, he started walking in the opposite direction. The host, once again, had to acknowledge Jonah was a real person and that this incident happened...but he said, once again, that it didn't happen like the Bible said. The Bible records this event as Jonah walking away and as he went in the wrong direction, he got on a boat to make sure he didn't head towards Nineveh. A big storm hit the boat and Jonah said the only way they would be saved is if they threw him overboard. They did exactly what he said as

fast as possible and threw his ass overboard. The minute

his body hit the water the storm stopped. The people on

the boat continued on their journey; while Jonah got

swallowed by a huge whale. The whale took Jonah back

towards Nineveh and when he got close enough to shore,

he spit Jonah up, Jonah walked his ass to shore and on to

Nineveh, delivered his message and that was the only

event we know of him. The host couldn't deny the

historical event, so he did what he did best and tried to

disprove it. According to him and other Bible scholars,

Jonah wasn't swallowed by a whale: he was abducted and

taken into an underwater submarine by a group of people

who lived underwater! Are you fucking kidding me!?!

That's the best you can come up with? You want to

disprove the Bible so badly, that you want to shift, shake

and move whatever you can in history to make sure

nothing happened the way the Bible said it did and I

fucking love it!!! Anyways, him and some other scholars

went on to 1ˢᵗ prove the existence of mermaids and an

underwater, human-like civilization and then they went

on to say it was them and their submarines that took

Jonah to Nineveh. Bullshit!

5. **Moses parting the Red Sea.** When the Israelites were at

the 1ˢᵗ leg of their exit from slavery in Egypt, they ran into

a little bit of a problem. That problem was the enormous

Red Sea. It is an actual body of water and the Israelites

actually were slaves in Egypt and during their exit, they

did run into the Red Sea. When they reached the sea,

word spread through their camp that the Egyptians had

changed their mind regarding freeing them and the

Pharoah had sent an elite army squad to hunt them down

and kill them or capture them and bring them back to

Egypt to be slaves again. The people began to get mad at

their leader, Moses. Moses in turn prays to God and asks

Him what should he do. God tells Moses to face towards

the Red Sea, raise the cane he had in his right hand and

the water would part down the middle so the Israelites

could walk through on dry ground! That's exactly what

happened and once they got to the other side, the

Egyptian army was coming around the corner in hot

pursuit. As they got further and further down the dry

path in the Red Sea, God made it close back up and

drowned the entire Egyptian force. Sounds crazy, right?

Well that's because it was a crazy and amazing event and

the hosts of the show, as crazy as the story was, could not

disprove it! They were aware it was another actual event

the Bible was recording and set out to show how God had

nothing to do with it. According to these nutjobs-with-

degrees, just at the right moment when the Israelites

needed to escape, the Red Sea was having a tidal

movement. If you're not familiar with tides, allow me to

crash-course you: water is at a certain level, but every

once in a while, based on the moon's distance from the

Earth, the moon's gravitational force has the ability to pull the edge of the water back, creating a new beachline of

sorts. These idiots are saying it just happened to be a

tidal movement that saved the Israelites, but unlike every

other tidal movement in history that pulled the shoreline

back, they want us to believe this was a once in a lifetime

tidal movement that, instead of pulling all the water back

from the shore, it decided to just form a clear tidal path

down the middle of the Red Sea that was large enough for

the Israelites to pass through! I call bullshit! I'm calling

bullshit and yes, I love it!!!

Alright, I hope I was able to show you with those examples

that being a Christian means you have a bullseye on your back

and you have to be able to see through the bullshit. You have to

see through the bullshit and understand it.

You have to understand it's not these documentary hosts

and media companies who want to disprove God...it's someone

behind them. They are just pawns and tools. The real enemy is a spiritual being named Satan. He is pulling the strings and it makes sense.

He is trying to prove God doesn't exist so that us humans deny the existence of God and become proud. We will think we are able to make our own laws about sex, money and everything else in life and that we're not accountable to anyone or anything.

This falls in to Satan's plan because now we are fighting for the right to kill our babies in the womb, we are taking prayer and the Bible out of our schools and introducing homosexual and transexual activity in to our schools; whatever goes against God and the Bible is being pushed on society and the media and science are the 2 main institutions being used.

Science is being used because science is supposed to be an arena based on facts and if Satan can twist scientific facts to show God doesn't exist...it will distract billions of humans away from God.

The media is being used because technology allows the media to reach everybody through cellphones, televisions, iPads and any electric device on the planet. We all know humans around the globe are now becoming more and more linked together through cellphones.

All Satan has to do is control the major media outlets and networks and he can get whatever message he wants to put out to the world in seconds to billions of people in every corner of the world. He is using science and science-based documentaries as a major venue for his bullshit and you have to keep your eyes open. Not your physical eyes...your spiritual eyes.

I've been curious and watched some of these shows and started to think some of it could, maybe, possibly have some truth to it until...until I looked at the information through my spiritual eyes. I'm encouraging anyone reading this to stay clear of the bullshit.

If you want to learn about some interesting Bible facts, stick with the Bible. If you want to expand your knowledge, did into the Lost Books of the Bible like the "Book of Enoch" and the "1st and 2nd Books of Adam and Eve" or the "Gospel of Thomas".

Anyone reading who doesn't believe Satan is real or that he has the ability to control science and the media, you have already been tricked! You already have been tricked and to un-trick yourself, I suggest the next book you read is, "You Tricked Me, Bitch! – a Human Story".

Yeah, that's a good place to stop. Just remember that you got the blood of a bull in your veins. You may be a sheep and led by the Good Shepherd, but on the inside, you're a bull and you need to act like it!

You need to be as aggressive with your spiritual walk as you possibly can and this starts with being able to recognize the bullshit and I'm here to help you as best I can, fellow bull!

Every book has some Private Matter Bonus Essays that relate to the book topic and this one is no different. These essays have topics people like to talk about in private, but get ashamed to talk about in public…I'm not.

I'm not and I think it's important to get this shit out here. Check a couple of 'em out:

JESUS FREAK

There is a term thrown around called "Jesus Freak". It was designed to be a put-down on anybody who was seriously into Jesus. It worked. Well, it worked for a little while. I have to admit, it even worked on me…at first.

Following the Bible and being a Christian has always been a social and religious target for people who want to live life on their own terms.

Nobody ever attacks Islam, Buddhism, Darwinism but if you mention you are a Christian or if you mention the name "Jesus", here come the sighs and the "why do you always have to talk about Jesus?" reactions.

Here's why. You know what? I was going to do it in paragraph form, but I just changed my mind. I like list's so I'm going to number some of the reasons why:

1.   Jesus is the only human who ever claimed to know God directly and He had plenty of supporting evidence with His actions.

2.   Jesus is the only human ever whose death was documented and witnessed by many people…and His resurrection was also witnessed and documented by many people.

3.   Jesus is the only human that had documented records where He was able to tell storms to die down and to control nature.

4.   Jesus is the only human who delivered a message that talked about getting personal with the creator of the Universe. All other religious and spiritual paths talk about some "thing" that is not designed for humans to get personal with (Islam being an exception...kind of).

5.   Jesus is the only human who is recorded as performing actual miracles. Miracles that included raising people from the dead.

6.   Jesus is the only human who gave us a clear explanation for human's purpose on Earth AND tied it into our spiritual origins. All other spiritual walks just tell us to do what we think is right and love everybody and we're gonna be A-ok.

7.   Jesus is the only human who has recorded and documented manuscripts written thousands of years before His birth that predicted His coming.

I could go on forever with this list, but I won't. I think you get the point that Jesus was and is an extraordinary individual. He spent His adult life here on Earth looking out for us. His laser-focus was to let us know that God is real, Satan and sin are real and that since He is the only one who actually witnessed Earth's beginnings and the rise and fall of Satan and sin, His goal was to teach us how to duplicate the Kingdom of Heaven here on Earth.

He also had a ton of lessons about life that, if followed properly, will make any individual find peace, happiness and success in every situation in life. He tied right, wrong, good, bad, God, Heaven, financial and spiritual wealth together in a way that no one before Him or since Him has been able to do.

If somebody wants to label me as a "Jesus Freak", I gladly accept that title. Actually, you can call me whatever the fuck you want to and I won't be offended or mad. In the case of the "Jesus Freak" label, I will actually shake your hand and thank you. That's a label I will gladly wear.

I have to say something about the "Jesus Freak" thing. A lot of people are finding it fashionable to wear bracelets that say "what would Jesus do" and people like to make social media posts that say "I love Jesus and He is My Lord and Savior. If you agree, please share." And now you got 3,000 mutha fuckas agreeing...but are they actually living like Jesus wants them to?

Do you remember the Lord's prayer? A lot of Believers say that prayer daily or at least a lot. How many of them understand that our purpose on Earth is to create Heaven on Earth? In that prayer, Jesus taught us to ask for "...may your Kingdom come..." That means we are asking for the Kingdom of Heaven to be established on Earth.

How does God work on Earth? Since He gave humans dominion, He rarely just comes in and does whatever He wants to do. He respects His own laws. What God looks for is for humans that He can work through.

The entire Bible if full of recorded events where God has Moses free the slaves, Joshua leading battles and prophets to give messages to world leaders and specific groups of people.

Jesus constantly told people who were interested in His lessons that they had to take action. Believers are supposed to suit up for spiritual warfare. Believers are supposed to stand up against laws that go directly against God's laws such as the legalization of homosexual marriage, corrupt and prejudicial drug sentencing laws and a host of other activity that certain members of society try and legalize so they can try and operate above God's laws.

A real "Jesus Freak" is ready to stand up when the rest of society is bowing down to social pressure. A "Jesus Freak" is an individual who doesn't just wear a *Jesus t-shirt* while he or she is actively involved in activities that destroy our temple such as drinking, vaping and letting their bodies get completely out of shape.

I will close with this: "Jesus Freaks" are the true leaders of society. Don't try and wear this badge without putting in the time. Being a "Jesus Freak" is not designed to be a fad. It involves daily prayer, meditation and conversations with our Heavenly Father, with Jesus and with the Holy Spirit.

The key word is "daily". A true "Jesus Freak" does not go to church one hour a week and think that their "God time" quota for the week is satisfied. You don't get to wear the "Jesus Freak" label if that's the only time you tryin' to put in.

"Jesus Freaks", it's time to run shit!!! It's time to stop being scared to stand up for shit!!!

It's time to stop letting human governments that contradict Heaven's government to continue to fuck shit up!!!

It's time to re-claim your lost shit!!! It's time to start a local Bible Fight Club!!!

It's time to do whatever your "Jesus" shirts are telling the

world that you do!!!

LET'S DO THIS SHIT FOR REAL, JESUS FREAKS!!!

I'll see the rest of you freaks at the finish line!!!

SALT and LIGHT

Salt and light are two of the most powerful and essential things on the planet. One has the ability to preserve things and the other has the power to expose things from fear to corruptions. Jesus said people who put His lessons into action should be the salt of the Earth and the light to the World. He wants His style of church to be a group of people with power and influence.

Jesus said the "Salt People" will be in charge of anything that deals with preserving the natural resources on Earth. Natural resources are not just steel, copper, plastic and water. It also includes human, animal and plant life. That means Salt People will need to do whatever they need to in order to hold any and all top positions that preserve the natural resources on Earth.

God instructed us to "maintain the Earth." This task ranges from recycling to protecting endangered wild life. It's not limited to those two tasks. They are just examples. The point is,

God needs people who want to be the Salt to maintain and

protect the Earth.

People who are destined to be the Light People have an

equally important role. They will be tasked with exposing

corruption in the world's systems. In general, light exposes things

and acts as a guide.

Whenever someone is in a dark place mentally, they need

some type of light.

Whenever a world system like finance and the media, are

operating and getting wealthy based on corruption and things

done in the dark, light needs to be shown on it to expose it.

Light People have the task of holding top positions of

power in the world systems of finance, business, media,

government, religion and education to keep corruption out. At

the same time, Light People will need to be able to guide people who are in dark places mentally. Maybe by sharing their

testimonies of how God brought them through dark times or

maybe by becoming psychologists and therapists.

Your walk in life as a Salt Person or a Light Person will be

ordained by God. What that process looks like will be different

for each person. Maybe you will be both…

Just know that Jesus said there will be a lot of people out

there who claim to want to follow Him…but the people who

actually walk the walk and talk the talk will be few…

Be a part of the few, the proud. And yes, the Marines got that

shit from Jesus.

The Church tells Believers that a personal relationship with God and Jesus is the ultimate goal. That's fine and all, but you can't say that and then not explain to us who God is because you think it's a tricky subject.

I've asked several people from pastors to old-timer Believers to please describe who God is. The best answer I've gotten is that He is a personality and so is Jesus and so is the Holy Spirit.

So, let me get this straight: my goal is to get personal with a personality that is somehow made up of 3 personalities? Not gonna happen. Impossible.

I don't know why the religious leaders avoid this subject so much. The more they ignore this important topic, the more I see why Jesus despised the religious leaders of His day. He was always getting into it with them and calling them snakes.

How about this: God is our Father and He is a Being. We are made in His image and He walks and talks and has arms and legs like us. He is NOT Jesus and when Jesus came to Earth, He was NOT God in an earthly body.

The Holy Spirit, God and Jesus are 3 separate Beings. Once I looked at like that, I was finally able to get personal with all 3 in our own way. And I have to admit it felt *extremely* good and my walk with them finally became a reality! I was able to tap into the Father-Son relationship with God by following the example Jesus gave us.

He was always talking about doing what His dad told Him to because He loves His dad and His dad loves Him. Viewing God as a 3-Being, shape-shifter will never get you to the point where you can get personal with Him because you can't get personal with a cloud.

The image of the holy trinity has helped Satan because it keeps us from getting a personal relationship with God. Jesus told us to pray to our Father who is in Heaven. That clearly means Him and God aren't the same Being. He also said, you can talk about me but anybody that talks about the Holy Spirit has committed the only sin that is unforgivable.

Moses was bold and asked God if he could see Him. God said that would be impossible because His glory is too bright. But He did tell Moses He would WALK past him and cover Moses up WITH HIS HANDS so he wouldn't try and look at God's face. God then said, I will uncover you so you can see my BACK as I WALK on to wherever He was headed.

There it is. God has a body, arms, back, legs and a face. Please get personal with Him on a one-on-one basis and stop believing the trinity teaching that God is a 3-Being personality or a

mysterious, impersonal "thing" that is made up of 3 other

"things."

Who's your daddy? God is!

Personal Development Notes

Personal Development Notes